CACTUS

CACTUS

by Cynthia Overbeck

Photographs by Shabo Hani

A Lerner Natural Science Book

Lerner Publications Company ▪ Minneapolis

Sylvia A. Johnson, Series Editor

Translation of original text by Chaim Uri

Additional research by Jane Dallinger

Drawing on page 28 by Kayo Takechi

The publisher wishes to thank Gary Lyons, Curator of Desert Plants, Huntington Library and Botanical Gardens, San Marino, California, for his assistance in the preparation of this book.

The glossary on page 46 gives definitions and pronunciations of words shown in **bold type** in the text.

LIBRARY OF CONGRESS CATALOGING IN PUBLICATION DATA

Overbeck, Cynthia.
  Cactus.

    (A Lerner natural science book)
    Adaptation of: Saboten no fushigi/Shabō Hani.
    Includes index.
    Summary: Describes the special parts of the cactus
  plant and how they work together to enable the plant
  to survive in the desert by storing water.
    1. Cactus—Juvenile literature. [1. Cactus. 2. Desert
  plants] I. Hani, Shabō, ill. II. Hani, Shabō. Saboten
  no fushigi. III. Title. IV. Series.

  QK495.C11093   583′.47   82-211
  ISBN 0-8225-1469-0 (lib. bdg.)   AACR2

This edition first published 1982 by Lerner Publications Company.
Text copyright © 1982 by Lerner Publications Company.
Photographs copyright © 1975 by Shabo Hani.
Adapted from THE MYSTERY OF CACTI copyright © 1975 by Shabo Hani.
English language rights arranged by Kurita-Bando Literary Agency
for Akane Shobo Publishers, Tokyo, Japan.

International Standard Book Number: 0-8225-1469-0
Library of Congress Catalog Card Number: 82-211

    2   3   4   5   6   7   8   9   10   91   90   89   88   87   86   85   84   83

It is noon in the American desert. Everything is still. Under the blazing sun, the baked ground is hard and dusty. It seems as if nothing can live in such burning heat and dryness. Yet dotting the landscape are tall, strange-looking shapes—columns of green with stiff, upturned arms. These are living plants—the huge saguaro cactus of the American Southwest.

They are just one of over 2,500 species, or different kinds, of cactus plants.

These hardy members of the family Cactaceae are native only to the Americas. They grow from southern Canada all the way down to Tierra del Fuego, at the tip of South America. The greatest variety of cactus plants are found in the deserts of the western and southwestern United States and northern Mexico.

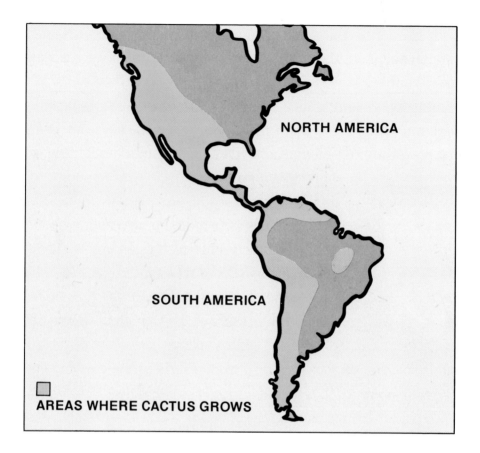

AREAS WHERE CACTUS GROWS

The desert is a place of contrasts. It is one of the earth's harshest, most barren regions. Yet it can also be a place of great beauty, full of plant and animal life. Some deserts are flat, empty stretches of sand where little but low bushes grow. Others lie in rocky foothills where many desert plants grow and bloom with bright flowers in the spring or autumn.

Even the temperatures of the desert may vary. Most people think of deserts as hot places. It is true that deserts in the southwestern United States and northern Mexico, for example, are hot. Their temperatures average 100°F (38°C) every day in summer. But some desert areas, such as those in eastern Oregon and Canada, are actually cold, reaching temperatures below freezing in winter. And even in the hot deserts, winter may bring snow.

Although the idea of a cold desert may seem strange, it is not extreme heat that makes a desert. It is dryness. A desert is any place where there is very little rainfall or where rainfall is unpredictable. Generally, the American deserts get an average of only 10 inches (25 centimeters) of rain a year. Sometimes a whole year or more can pass without any rainfall at all. In contrast, a place with more rainfall—Iowa, for example—gets an average of 31.5 inches (78 centimeters) of rain every year.

Because of the lack of rain, the air in the desert is usually very dry. There is very little humidity, or moisture, in the air, and there are rarely clouds in the sky. Nothing shields the desert earth or its inhabitants from the sun's fierce, burning rays.

When rain does come to the desert, it is usually in the form of short, violent cloudbursts and thunderstorms. So much rain falls all at once that the desert earth, which has been baked hard by the sun, cannot soak it up. Often there are flash floods. Much of the precious rainwater runs off into channels that lead it away from the desert.

Left: **A baseball plant from southwestern Africa.** *Below:* **The common hen-and-chicken plant.**

A plant that can survive under such extreme conditions must be hardy indeed. The cactus is just such a plant. It survives in the desert because of its unique ability to store water.

Any plant that can store an extra supply of water is known as a **succulent.** Succulents have special roots, stems, or leaves that act almost like sponges to soak up and hold whatever moisture they receive. Many kinds of succulent plants grow in dry areas throughout the world. Some, like the hen-and-chickens plant, store water in their thick, juicy leaves. Others, like the baseball plant of southwestern Africa, store water in their fat stems.

The stem of a cactus often looks fat and swollen with water.

Cactus plants are succulents that store most of their water supply in the fleshy tissue of their stems. The main part of a cactus plant is its heavy stem. Scattered over the stem's surface are clusters of sharp **spines** growing from little raised discs called **areoles**. Only a true cactus has spines arranged in this way. Succulents like the baseball plant are similar to cactus in other ways, but they do not have spines growing from areoles.

All the special parts of a cactus—its stem and spines as well as its roots and thick outer skin, or **epidermis**—play an important part in helping the cactus to live in the desert's dry heat. The story of how these parts develop and then work together is a fascinating one.

A cactus sprout pushes its way above ground.

Although cactus plants may look strange and exotic, they are related to such familiar plants as the sunflower, the rose, and the apple tree. All are flowering plants, and all develop in the same basic way.

Like other flowering plants, almost all cactus plants grow from seeds. A cactus seed must have water and food in order to sprout. It may lie in the dry desert earth for a year or more, waiting for enough moisture. When at least ¾ inch (20 millimeters) of rain falls at one time, the seed will sprout.

Under the ground, a tiny, thread-like root begins to grow out of the seed and down into the earth. Above the ground, two special leaves, called **cotyledons,** push through. Cotyledons are thick leaves that contain food stored in the seed. This food will feed the new cactus sprout in the early stages of its growth.

Left: The black seed covering remains attached to the cotyledons. *Right:* The cotyledons spread apart.

As the cotyledons grow above ground, roots are developing below. The roots hold the plant firmly in the ground. They also take in water and minerals from the soil.

Some cactus plants have a main root that extends as much as 15 feet (1.5 meters) down into the earth to reach water. Others have roots that spread out in a wide, shallow network. In large cactus plants, such roots may grow as far as 50 feet (18 meters) out from the main plant. These roots can soak up water from even a light rain that doesn't penetrate the ground very deeply.

The cactus sprout gets its first spines.

With roots growing below the ground and cotyledons above, the new cactus seems to be developing in much the same way as other green plants. But soon, the cactus sprout will take a different course. Instead of the tiny green leaves that most young plants develop, little spines begin to grow between the two cotyledons.

Soon after the first spines appear, the cactus stem also begins to develop between the cotyledons. As the stem becomes bigger and thicker, spines start to grow out of its areoles. It is not long before the little cactus is covered with a coat of sharp spines.

Spines play an important part in helping a cactus to survive in the desert. A dense covering of spines actually helps to shade the cactus stem from the sun's rays. The spines do this by filtering the light in much the same way that a slatted shade does. Sharp spines also protect the cactus from many desert animals. Otherwise, the stem would be a juicy meal for thirsty rodents and cattle.

This little cactus is well protected by a coat of sharp spines.

Fire barrel cactus

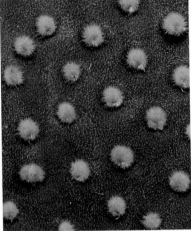

Close-up of a bunny ears cactus

Peruvian old woman cactus

Although all cactus spines have the same basic uses, the spines of various kinds of cactus plants can look very different. Some are like a cluster of straight, sharp needles. Others look soft and fluffy, like cotton candy. Often cactus spines are brightly colored. These pictures show several different kinds of cactus spines.

Rainbow cactus

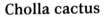

Cholla cactus

In addition to regular spines, some cactus have tiny, sharp bristles called **glochids**. Clusters of these bristles grow out of the areoles just as the spines do. Glochids have little barbs on them, and they will stick to almost anything that brushes against them.

The cholla (CHOY-uh) and the prickly pear are two kinds of cactus that have glochids as well as spines.

Spines

Areole

Glochids

Left: This drawing shows how glochids grow on a prickly pear cactus. *Right:* The cholla is another kind of cactus with glochids as well as spines.

Above: Prickly pear cactus.
Left: Silver torch cactus.

Just as cactus plants have different kinds of spines, they also have stems of different shapes and sizes. The silver torch cactus grows in tall, slender columns, while the stem of the tiny pincushion cactus looks like a little round ball. The prickly pear has a stem made up of flat, jointed sections. In periods of extreme dryness, the jointed parts sometimes drop off the plant to save water.

Above left: **Pincushion cactus.** *Above right:*
Barrel cactus. *Right:* **Living rock cactus.**

One of the strangest kinds of cactus are those known as living rocks. Grey and withered in appearance, they do look more like rocks than green plants. Yet they grow and live like other cactus.

Cactus stems not only have different shapes but also different textures and surfaces. The stems of the silver torch, the saguaro, and the barrel cactus have alternating ribs and grooves running from top to bottom. The many spines on these cactus plants grow from rows of areoles along the raised ribs.

Other kinds of cactus have stems covered with bumps called **tubercules**. Each tubercule is tipped with an areole and spines. In the picture of the pincushion cactus on this page, you can clearly see the tubercules with their spiny tips.

● The saguaro is the giant of the desert. A full-grown saguaro cactus can be as tall as 25 feet (around 7 meters) and can weigh up to 6 tons (5.4 metric tons). A whole forest of these amazing plants grows in the Saguaro National Monument in Arizona.

All of these cactus stems—tall or short, slender or round, ribbed or bumpy—are specially made to store water. Inside, they are composed of tissues that soak up and hold water almost like a sponge. The stored water in a cactus stem may make up as much as 90 percent of the plant's weight. In many kinds of cactus, the whole stem swells when full of water. A six-ton (5.4-metric-ton) saguaro can take in up to one ton (.9 metric tons) of water. When full, its main stem may swell a foot (30 centimeters) or more in thickness.

Just as the cactus swells when full of water, it shrinks and shrivels when its water supply is low. The grooves between the ribs or tubercules sink in, and the raised parts stick out.

In addition to storing water, the stem is the cactus plant's food-making center. Like all green plants, a cactus must have nourishment as well as water in order to grow. After the food stored in the seed is used up, all plants, including the cactus, must make their own food. In most plants, food is made in the leaves. The leaves take in light energy from the sun. They also take in the gas carbon dioxide and water from the air. At the same time, the leaves receive more water and minerals from the roots. The sun's energy combines the carbon dioxide, water, and minerals to make a kind of plant sugar that is changed into food.

Left: The barrel cactus in the picture at the top hasn't been watered for two years, yet it is still alive. A cross-section cut from this cactus (bottom picture) shows how its tissues are shriveled and its ribs stick out. *Right:* These two pictures show a well-watered barrel cactus with a fat stem and water-filled tissues.

In the leafless cactus, the stem does the job of making food. As in other plants, a cactus stem has tiny rod-like structures inside it. These structures are called **vascular bundles.** They carry water and minerals up from the roots and throughout the stem. The stem also takes in carbon dioxide and water from the air through its epidermis. Food is then made in the same way that it is made in other plants.

While they are making food, all plants are constantly giving off water and gases as well as taking them in. Plant leaves have many tiny openings on their surfaces through which these substances enter and leave. Leafy plants have large numbers of such openings, which are called **stomata.** The leaf of a morning glory plant, for example, may have 62,500 stomata per square inch (10,000 per square centimeter).

Left: **A morning glory leaf.** *Right:* **A magnified view of the leaf surface, showing the oval-shaped stomata.**

In many plants, large amounts of water are given off through the stomata in a process called **transpiration.** A small fruit tree, for example, might lose up to 300 quarts (285 liters) of water on a hot day. In a climate with normal rainfall, this water is always being replaced. But in the dry desert, a plant that loses so much water could not survive.

The cactus survives because it can hold most of the water it takes in rather than giving it off. Of course, most cactus plants have no leaves through which to lose water. They do have stomata on their stems, but there are no more than 2,500 of these openings per square inch (400 per square centimeter). So the transpiration rate—the rate at which water is given off—is very slow. On a hot day, a large saguaro may lose only about a cup of water. A cactus's thick epidermis, which is covered with a waxy coating, also helps to slow down transpiration.

A magnified view of the epidermis of a cactus. There are many fewer stomata than on the morning glory leaf.

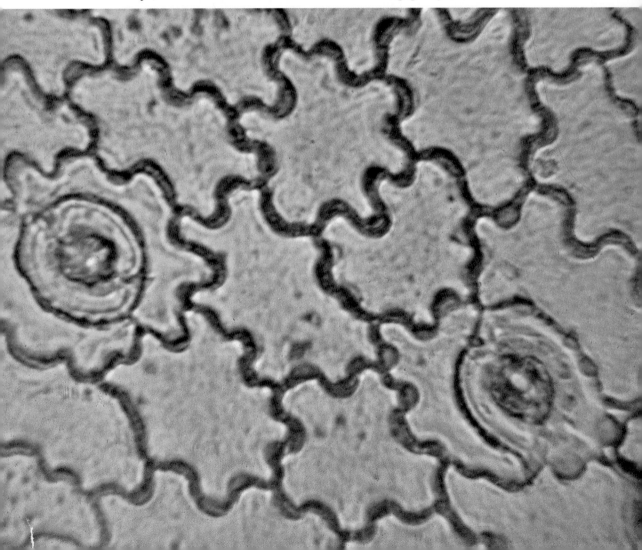

This picture shows two types of barrel cactus. The small plants with red spines are fire barrels, and behind them are several golden barrels. Both kinds have single stems with no branches.

This owl's eyes cactus
has a divided stem.

With enough water, sunlight, and minerals from the soil, a cactus will produce the food that it needs to grow. Most cactus plants grow very slowly. The giant saguaros may take more than 100 years to become mature. Once grown, they may live for 200 years or more. Many other types of cactus live for at least 20 years.

Different kinds of cactus plants have different ways of growing larger. Some, like the saguaro and the cholla, produce branches that sprout from the main stem. The growth of other kinds of cactus takes place on the main stem itself. Some types of barrel cactus, like those shown in the picture on the opposite page, grow by adding more ribs. They get larger and fatter, but they don't grow any branches.

A few kinds of cactus, especially those with tubercules, grow whole new stems every year. The original stem divides in two at the top so that two identical stems are growing side by side. Each year, the stems multiply.

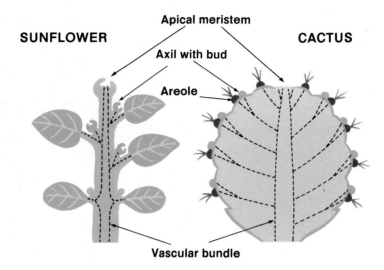

SUNFLOWER   Apical meristem   CACTUS

Axil with bud

Areole

Vascular bundle

When cactus stems multiply or grow taller, the growth takes place at a point on the tip of the stem called the **apical meristem.** The stems of other flowering plants like sunflowers also grow from an apical meristem.

Branches grow from a different point on a plant. In most flowering plants, they grow from the **axil.** In plants with leaves, this is the point that lies in the upper angle formed where a leaf is attached to the stem. Among cactus plants, the axil point may be in one of several different places. For example, in a branching cactus with ribs, like the toothpick cactus pictured on the opposite page, the branches grow from a point just above the areoles. In most other kinds of cactus, the branches arise directly from the areoles.

28

Bright pink flowers bloom on two kinds of pincushion cactus.

As a cactus continues to grow, it eventually develops to the point where it is ready to produce flowers. Some types of cactus will flower a year or two after sprouting; others take several years or even longer.

When cactus plants flower, the desert is transformed. A landscape that was dusty green and brown comes alive with brilliant red, pink, and yellow flowers. These beautiful flowers have an important job to do. They must produce seeds from which new cactus plants will grow.

A cactus flower begins as a **bud**—a tight ball of petals and flower parts. The flower buds usually grow from the same point on a cactus plant as branches do. In a cactus with ribs, the flowers bloom on the ribs, from within or next to the areoles. In a cactus with tubercules, the flowers bloom in the spaces between the tubercules.

30

The developing bud of a cactus plant is protected from the hot sun by a thick skin covered with small spines or a thick mat of hairs. This covering also protects the bud from damage by insects and animals.

The flower bud of a hedgehog cactus. It has been cut open to show the tightly bunched yellow anthers clustered around the pistil. The green stigmas are at the top of the pistil; the rounded ovary is at the bottom.

THE PARTS OF A CACTUS FLOWER

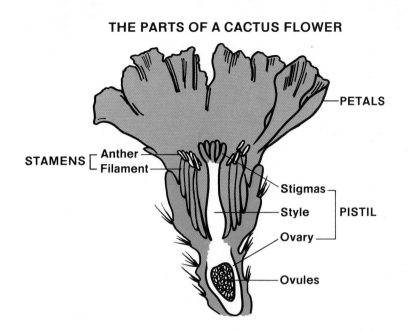

The flower that develops inside the bud has a structure much like that of other flowers. The petals are joined together at the base to form a kind of tube. Within the tube are male and female parts that work together to make seeds. In the center is the **pistil,** or female part. At its base is a kind of hollow sac called the **ovary.** Inside the ovary are many tiny **ovules.** Each contains an egg cell that will grow into a seed. A **style,** or small stalk, grows out of the ovary. At its top is an opening surrounded by a ring of **stigmas.**

Clustered around the pistil are many **stamens**—the male parts of the flower. Each stamen is made up of a **filament,** or thin stalk, topped by an **anther.** The anthers are filled with **pollen,** a powdery yellow substance that contains male sperm cells.

33

Opposite: The flower of a hedgehog cactus in full bloom. It has been cut open to show the inside. *Right:* The stigmas of a hedgehog cactus flower ready to receive pollen.

In order for seeds to grow in the ovary, sperm cells from the anthers must fertilize, or unite with, egg cells in the ovules. But first, pollen containing the sperm must reach the stigmas.

The stigmas of most cactus flowers are made in such a way that they cannot receive pollen from the anthers right next to them. Pollen must come instead from another cactus plant of the same species. This can happen only with help from the animal world.

Birds, bats, and insects that live in the desert like to eat the sweet nectar produced by cactus flowers. The bright colors of the flowers attract these animals to the sweet meal that waits for them.

As an insect, bird, or bat moves over a flower gathering nectar, pollen from the anthers rubs off on its body. When it flies to a new flower, the pollen rubs off onto that flower's stigmas. Some of the grains of pollen split open and send long **pollen tubes** down the style and into the ovary. Tiny sperm cells then drop down the tubes. They come together with the egg cells in the ovules, and the eggs are fertilized. When this happens, seeds begin to grow in the ovary.

The cactus reproduces in the same basic way as other flowering plants, but because of the harsh desert environment, its method of reproduction must be more efficient. The large number of stamens in a cactus flower (around 3,400 on one saguaro flower) insures a huge supply of pollen. The large, bright cactus flowers attract many pollinators, so the pollen is sure to be spread around. Once a flower is pollinated, the large number of ovules in a single ovary helps to make sure that there will be many seeds. This is important because a large percentage of seeds will never sprout. They may die from lack of water, or birds and mice may eat them. Many seeds must be produced so that a few will survive.

Large bright flowers like that of the hedgehog cactus attract
many pollinating insects and birds.

Most cactus flowers live for only a few days. Some, like those of the queen of the night cactus, bloom only at night and live for less than 24 hours. Because of their short life spans, cactus flowers do not use too much precious water and quickly complete the important job of producing seeds.

38

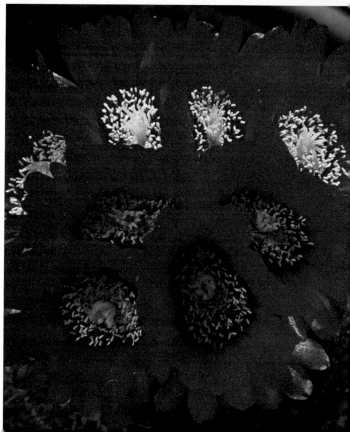

The pictures on these two pages show flowers from several different cactus plants. *Opposite:* Lady finger cactus. *Above left:* Queen of the night cactus. *Above right:* Easter lily cactus. *Right:* Crimson parodia cactus.

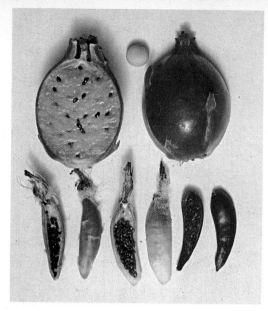

This picture shows different kinds of cactus fruits. At the top is the fleshy fruit of a climbing cactus, cut open to show the seeds. (Between the two halves is a soybean for comparison of size.) The capsule-like fruits at the bottom are from a pincushion cactus.

As the seeds grow, the petals, anthers, and other parts of the flower wither and dry up. Some types of cactus develop a special protective covering around the seeds. This covering and the seeds inside are called the **fruit**.

There are many different kinds of cactus fruits. Most are juicy and fleshy, while some are more like dry capsules. Cactus fruits can be long and thin or round and fat. They range in color from bright red to pale green, yellow, or white.

When the fruit is ripe and the seeds are ready to grow on their own, the cactus plant again gets help from the animal world. Birds and small animals often eat cactus fruit, and in doing so, they help to scatter the seeds.

Sometimes animals eat the flesh of the cactus fruit and simply drop the seeds on the ground. Sometimes they eat the whole fruit, seeds and all. The seeds pass through their digestive systems unharmed and drop to the ground.

The strange-looking fruits of this pincushion cactus are called "chillitos." They are sweet and edible.

After cactus seeds have been scattered on the ground, they must wait for enough moisture in order to sprout. Some seeds may sprout right away, while others may have to wait a year or more until a heavy rain soaks the dry ground. But sooner or later, some seeds will sprout and grow. Then these new cactus plants will replace those that have grown old or are damaged.

Cactus plants are very important to the life of the desert. Full-grown cactus plants often provide the only shade from the hot desert sun—shade that young plants and small animals need to survive. Many birds make their nests in the stems of a large cactus like the saguaro. Birds, bats, and insects eat cactus flower nectar. Many animals eat the fruit and sometimes even the fleshy stems.

Human beings also find uses for cactus plants. People living in the desert have traditionally eaten the fruits and seeds of some kinds of cactus. They have also used the curved spines of the fishhook cactus for catching fish. And many people all over the world like to grow unusual and beautiful cactus plants in their gardens or houses.

Fishhook cactus

Unfortunately, this last use has created problems for the future of the cactus. Because there is such a great demand for these plants, many people have gone into the business of digging up cactus plants in the desert and selling them. Although states like California, Arizona, and New Mexico have strict laws against removing cactus plants from the desert, many "cactus thieves" take them anyway.

Today there are 27 kinds of cactus on the endangered species list, and the number is growing. Environmentalists are working to get stricter laws passed to protect the cactus and to set aside special areas where the plants can grow undisturbed. People are also being encouraged to buy only cactus plants that are raised from seed instead of plants dug up in the desert. If these efforts are not successful, then some kinds of cactus may become extinct and an important part of natural life could be lost forever.

GLOSSARY

anther—the part of a flower's stamen that contains pollen

areole (AWR-ee-uhl)—the area on a cactus stem or branch where spines grow

apical meristem (AY-pih-kuhl MER-ih-stem)—the growing point at the top of a plant stem

axil (AK-suhl)—the angle formed above a leaf or spine at the point where it joins a stem or branch

bud—a small swelling on a plant from which a leaf, stem, or flower develops

cotyledon (kaht-'l-EED-un)—a special leaf containing stored food from the seed

epidermis (eh-pih-DERM-is)—the outer skin of a plant

fertilization—the uniting of a male sperm cell and female egg cell to produce a seed

filament—the stalk of a stamen

fruit—the protective structure that develops around the seeds of flowering plants

glochids (GLOW-kids)—fine, sharp bristles that grow in clusters on some types of cactus plants

nectar (NECK-tuhr)—a sweet liquid produced by flowers that attracts insects, birds, and bats

ovary—the part of the pistil in which seeds grow

ovule (OH-vyool)—the tiny structure in the pistil that grows into a seed

pistil—the seed-producing part of a flower

pollen—a powdery substance containing male sperm cells

pollen tube—a tiny tube that carries sperm cells from a pollen grain into the ovary of a flower

spines—sharp stickers or bristles on a cactus

stamen (STAY-mehn)—the pollen-producing part of a flower

stigma—the part of the pistil that receives pollen

stomata (STO-muh-tuh)—tiny openings in the epidermis of a leaf or stem through which water and gases pass in and out. The singular form of the word is *stoma.*

style (STILE)—the narrow part of the pistil that supports the stigmas

succulent (SUK-yuh-lunt)—any plant with special roots, stems, or leaves that can store large amounts of water over a period of time

transpiration—the giving off of water from a green plant's leaves or stem

tubercules (TEW-bur-kuhls)—lumpy or knobby projections on some types of cactus, tipped with areoles and spines

vascular bundle (VAS-kyuh-luhr)—a kind of tube or rod that carries water and minerals through a plant's stem

INDEX